THE PRISONER

OTHER BOOKS BY PETER BROOK
PUBLISHED BY TCG

Evoking (and Forgetting) Shakespeare

The Quality of Mercy *Reflections on Shakespeare*

The Shifting Point *Theatre, Film, Opera 1946–1987*

Conversations with Peter Brook *1970–2000*
(Interviews with Margaret Croyden)

THE PRISONER

Peter Brook

and

Marie-Hélène Estienne

THEATRE COMMUNICATIONS GROUP
NEW YORK
2018

The Prisoner is published by Theatre Communications Group, Inc.
520 Eighth Avenue, 24th Floor, New York, NY 10018-4156

This volume is published in arrangement with Nick Hern Books Limited,
The Glasshouse, 49a Goldhawk Road, London W12 8QP

This publication is made possible in part by the New York State Council on
the Arts with the support of Governor Andrew Cuomo and the New York
State Legislature.

TCG books are exclusively distributed to the book trade by Consortium
Book Sales and Distribution.

A catalogue record for this book is available from the Library of Congress.

ISBN 978-1-55936-957-2 (paperback)

Front cover photo of Kalieaswari Srinivasan from the original production
of *The Prisoner* by Simon Annand

First TCG Edition, November 2018

Introduction

Peter Brook and Marie-Hélène Estienne

Somewhere in the world a man is sitting alone in front of a prison.

Who is he? Why is he sitting there in front of a prison? Is it a deliberate choice? Is it a punishment? As for those who are inside, what crime have they committed? And what do they think of that man, facing them, free? Is he mad? Is he a fanatic? A criminal? What punishment for what crime?

What sort of justice is this? Who decided it? The man himself? Why is he allowed to stay there? These are questions for those who control the prison, and for those who are locked up. Is the man looking for redemption? Has he visitors? Is he tempted to run away?

In *The Prisoner* we are attempting to penetrate the richness of all these themes.

July 2018

The Prisoner was first performed at Théâtre des Bouffes du Nord, Paris, on 6 March 2018, with the following cast:

Hiran Abeysekera
Ery Nzaramba
Omar Silva
Kalieaswari Srinivasan
Donald Sumpter

Writers and Directors	Peter Brook
	and Marie-Hélène Estienne
Lighting	Philippe Vialatte
Set Elements	David Violi
Costume Assistant	Alice François
With thanks to	Tarell Alvin McCraney
	and Alexander Zeldin

It was a production of C.I.C.T. – Théâtre des Bouffcs du Nord, Paris, in a co-production with the National Theatre of Great Britain; the Grotowski Institute, Wrocław; Ruhrfestspiele Recklinghausen; Yale Repertory Theatre, New Haven; and Theatre for a New Audience, New York.

The production received its British premiere at the Royal Lyceum Theatre Edinburgh, as part of the Edinburgh International Festival, on 22 August 2018, before transferring to the Dorfman auditorium of the National Theatre, London, on 12 September 2018.

The Prisoner was performed at Theatre for a New Audience on November 24, 2018, with the following cast:

Hiran Abeysekera
Hayley Carmichael
Herve Goffings
Omar Silva
Kalieaswari Srinivasan

Writers and Directors	Peter Brook
	and Marie-Hélène Estienne
Lighting	Philippe Vialatte
Set Elements	David Violi
Costume Assistant	Alice François
With thanks to	Tarell Alvin McCraney
	and Alex Zeldin

It was a production of C.I.C.T. – Théâtre des Bouffes du Nord, Paris, in a co-production with the National Theatre of Great Britain; the Grotowski Institute, Wroclaw; Ruhrfestspiele Recklinghausen; Yale Repertory Theatre, New Haven; and Theatre for a New Audience, New York.

THE PRISONER

CHARACTERS

VISITOR
WOMAN
EZEKIEL
NADIA
MAVUSO
GUARD
FATHER, *voice-over*
MAN
GUARD 1
GUARD 2

1.

VISITOR. I was for a while in a faraway country. Its capital in those days had magic, not the dreamlike magic of white walls and perfumes, but a rough brown magic, brown like the mud walls and the mud lanes, a magic of this world, rude and hard, enhanced by the quality of its people.

Once, walking in the market, I passed an old cobbler sitting cross-legged in his stall, pouring tea. As his hand was moving the cup to his lips, in an unbroken gesture, his movement changed its direction, and the cup was held out to me, an offering that was the natural answer to my indiscreet stare.

Another time I saw a dwarf sitting motionless. As I passed I paused to observe him from the corner of my eye. Long after his image remained with me as the embodiment of strength. For he was a man accepting totally who he was, where he was, what he was. A dwarf in infinity, like us all.

I heard about a remarkable man, whose name was Ezekiel – like the prophet in the Bible. His house was hidden in the very heart of the market, and one day I found myself knocking at his door. A young woman opened and said –

WOMAN. He is not yet back. Please come in.

VISITOR. I waited and waited. Afternoon became evening, tea was brought, the sun went down, and night fell. And suddenly he was there.

EZEKIEL. You look as though you come from afar. How can I help you?

VISITOR. I answered with my eternal question… How to respond to the obscure intimations we have that beyond the everyday world there is in life something else.
I went on – using a metaphor – In me there are many rooms, crammed with a jumble of unnecessary objects. He seemed to understand me, so I continued: Occasionally I seem to hear sounds. I don't know where they come from, or what they are…

EZEKIEL. What sort of sounds? Could they come from the pipes? Have you called in a plumber?

VISITOR. I thought that he was making fun of me. But I realised that he was a practical man and was accustomed to giving practical advice.

When he heard that I was going to see an extraordinary forest with the most ancient trees, he told me –

EZEKIEL. I know that forest very well. In the middle of your journey you will cross a desert, in that desert you will see a huge white building, this is a prison. You will stop and walk up a hill. There, you will see a young man sitting, facing the prison. He is my nephew. His name is Mavuso. He has committed an unspeakable crime. Go and tell him I sent you.

VISITOR. Why was that man sitting in front of a prison? Why did Ezekiel ask me to go and see him? And what was the unspeakable crime?

2.

In EZEKIEL*'s house – years before.*

A young woman, NADIA, *is speaking to her uncle*
EZEKIEL.

EZEKIEL. Nadia, what are doing here, in the middle of
the night?

NADIA. Tonight Mavuso came into Father's house, he
found us in bed together, in one another's arms. He
grabbed a statue and smashed Father's head. Father is
lying on the ground, dead.

At this moment there is a knock on the door –

MAVUSO. It's me, Mavuso! Please, Uncle Ezekiel, let
me in!

The door opens. In a corner of the room, on her knees,
NADIA, MAVUSO*'s sister, tries to be invisible.*

EZEKIEL. Your sister told me what happened – Perhaps
you want to tell me more.

MAVUSO *doesn't answer – He stares at his sister.*

3.

Punishment.

MAVUSO *is lying on the earth. Above him* EZEKIEL *is holding a long pointed stick. He pierces* MAVUSO*'s thighs.*

EZEKIEL. You have murdered your father. This is the punishment you deserve, if you survive, you will still need to be punished.

He goes away, leaving MAVUSO *bleeding on the ground.*

4.

MAVUSO *is still on the ground. His legs are infected.*
NADIA *arrives. She covers his thighs with ointment.*

5.

MAVUSO *comes back home*. EZEKIEL *is waiting for him, with a* GUARD.

EZEKIEL. I tried to punish you in our traditional way. Nadia cured you. I hoped that you would leave and find a new place elsewhere. But I knew that you would come back and I was waiting for you. Now you have to be tried, and judged.

MAVUSO. I came back because I want to be judged.

MAVUSO *leaves with the* GUARD, *handcuffed*.

6.

The GUARD *puts* MAVUSO *in a tiny cell.*

GUARD. Here is your new home for twenty years of isolation. I hope you'll like it.

He closes the door.

Enjoy!

MAVUSO *is lying on the floor trying to sleep when he hears, from different sides, knocks and taps. He starts to answer and gradually the taps become like a dialogue.*

7.

The GUARD *opens the door of the cell.*

GUARD. You have a visitor. Come with me.

8.

MAVUSO *and* NADIA *are facing each other.*

NADIA. It has been very difficult to come here, they did not want to let me in. But I succeeded. Mavuso, I have something very important to tell you.

MAVUSO. I have also something very important to tell you – I love you. I always loved you. I love you in the way Father loved you, and you know it.

NADIA. And you killed him. I loved Father. He did not force me. You know that too. Here is what I wanted to tell you, I'm pregnant.

MAVUSO. I think it's better if you leave. Guard, come here, show her out.

NADIA *leaves.*

The GUARD *comes to* MAVUSO.

GUARD. Who do you think you are? 'Guard, come here! Guard, come here!'

You're transferred, father-killer, they should have put you in the pit, but instead they transfer you. God knows why! I'm sure that in the other place they'll make your life a hell, vermin.

9.

Outside MAVUSO *finds* EZEKIEL, *waiting for him.*

MAVUSO. What are you doing here?

EZEKIEL. I'm taking you.

MAVUSO. Where to?

EZEKIEL. Come.

10.

They are now in a forest.

EZEKIEL. You remember this forest? We used to come here when you were a child. I showed you all that the forest contains.

Where is the sacred tree?

MAVUSO *finds the tree*.

Your father, whenever he felt soiled, used to come and sit under that tree. After five days without eating nor drinking, he would leave completely cleansed. He showed it to me at first. And I sat there too, many times, without drinking and eating. I showed it to you, though I never told you about its power. I tried to explain to you that your father had more knowledge than me, but you closed your ears.

MAVUSO *wants to sit under the sacred tree*.

No, you're not ready for that. At my request, the judge has agreed to change your sentence. You will not see a forest for a very long time. It's why I brought you here. I want you to be able to keep that inside you. It will help you.

Take your time, I'll be waiting for you.

11.

They are in a desert. There are only twigs, burnt trees, stones and earth.

EZEKIEL *carries a bag and leaves it on the ground.*

EZEKIEL. Mavuso, you have inside you many possibilities. I could not bear to have you in prison, isolated, rotting, like a beast waiting to be slaughtered. So I spoke to the judge. He was your father's best friend. And he accepted my request.

You'll stay here, without a cell, without bars, with always the temptation to leave, facing the prison that is in front of us, for the duration of your sentence.

Don't say anything.

They face the prison in silence. Then MAVUSO *opens the bag. There are some clothes, some matches, some water, a plate and a big black book.*

MAVUSO. Father's book!

EZEKIEL. A reminder. If someone asks you – as you will never be really alone – if someone asks you: Why are you here? you'll reply: I am here to repair.

Tonight I will sleep here but in the morning I'll be gone. Then it will be up to you.

12.

When MAVUSO *wakes up,* EZEKIEL *is gone. He starts to prepare a little space for himself.*

When he has finished, he sits facing the prison for a long while. Lights arise, lights fade, lights come back, lights fade and come back again.

13.

MAVUSO *opens the book that has been left on the ground.*

Suddenly the FATHER *appears.*

MAVUSO. Father!

FATHER (*voice-over*). There is a very special and sacred tree. From its bark we extract a juice. When someone has committed a crime he is put in front of that sacred tree – but the juice the tree is producing is poisoned – The murderer has to drink that poison – He usually dies, there is no way out – but sometimes the poison has no action on him, and he can go back to his life.

14.

MAVUSO. Why did I do it? Was I jealous? Why couldn't I respect him? Why that hatred? He never did anything against me. He seemed to love me. I was his son. He wanted to protect me.

And Nadia – why do I love my sister? Why did my heart break for her? Why? I think about her day and night.

Should I leave this place? – Should I rush to the door of the prison and ask to be let in – At least there I could feel the punishment that I deserve and for which I have been justly sentenced – Here I cannot feel it! Here I feel nothing.

15.

MAVUSO *lights a fire, and starts to eat.*

A rat arrives, looking for food – MAVUSO *shares his food with the rat. They eat slowly. It is night,* MAVUSO *lies on the ground, the rat in his arms.*

During the night the rat starts biting him violently. MAVUSO *has no choice. He kills him. He cries –*

MAVUSO. Why did I kill again? I loved him, he gave me warmth.

He cooks the rat and eats it.

16.

A MAN *with a gun appears, he points it at* MAVUSO.

MAN. You must go, you are a troublemaker, we, in the village, we thought that you will leave, but it's now three months that you are here, you take our water, we saw you, we said nothing, we were sure that soon you'd be gone. Now that cannot go on. This earth is not yours, it belongs to us – You spoil it with your excrement. And now you are eating our country rat, you must go!

MAVUSO. I do not know if I killed the rat, I do not know if he was real, I do not know if I ate him. And I cannot go. Impossible.

There is something so pathetic in MAVUSO*'s expression that the* MAN *is deeply touched. He sits next to him, puts the gun on the ground, looks at him.*

MAN. Tell me: why are you here? For so long you've spoken to no one. The man with the car never came back. It is very hard for you to find food, and water, you have no help, why are you here, facing the prison? Why?

MAVUSO. I am here to repair.

MAN. Repair? Repair what? I'll come back and you'll speak!

The MAN *starts to go away.*

MAVUSO. What is your name?

MAN. I am the man from the village. And you, what is your name?

MAVUSO. Mavuso, the man on the hill.

17.

One night two GUARDS *appear while* MAVUSO *is sleeping, he opens his eyes and see two faces bending over him.*

GUARD 2. We watched you, waking up and praying to the sun.

GUARD 1. The governor of the prison wants to get rid of you.

GUARD 2. The prisoners, they see you all the time, you cannot see them, but they see you, they talk about you all day long.

GUARD 1. You are disturbing the system! We are bored, the prisoners are boring. The director is boring. Our job is boring!

GUARD 2. Now they have added some political prisoners, it's worse, there are too many of them, not a single corner without a body. We have too much work. It's only today that we found the time to come and check what's going on here.

GUARD 1. They commit suicide, and we are supposed to prevent them. But they go on and we are blamed. We need to have some fun.

Look what I have here!

He shows a bottle of alcohol. They drink together, they sing some songs,

Listen. I will tell you a story.

A man wakes up with a huge erection. He runs to the whorehouse. The madam welcomes him with a smile – Here we have plenty of girls, small, tall, skinny, fat, you can take your pick… The man shakes his head – It's not what I want. Oh I see, we have also young men, big, small, He shakes his head. It's not what I want. The lady seems to understand and adds – We have animals – goats – dogs – we also have a donkey. The man says It's not what I want. The madam is puzzled – So what do you want? The man says – What have you got in fish? –

The sun starts to rise, the GUARDS *leave quickly to go back to their work. They leave the bottle for* MAVUSO, *who goes on drinking, and laughing to himself.*

18.

The MAN *from the village comes back. He wakes up*
MAVUSO.

MAN. It's time for you to go. You are young, you can
work, you can earn your living, the only thing you do
here is burn in the sun, and getting drunk, that will not
get you anywhere.

MAVUSO *drinks some water and says nothing.*

MAN. You want to stay here? Okay. I'll leave you, but
know that I will always come back. I won't let you die
alone.

A young woman has been seen in the village, she is
looking for a Mavuso. She is looking for you! Her
name is Nadia. She is very beautiful.

MAVUSO*'s eyes burn – the* MAN *sees something in
them that he did not see before –*

It's because of her?

19.

NADIA *arrives*.

NADIA. A little girl is born. She is three now. She found some pictures of you. They never leave her. You must come and live with us. She needs a father.

MAVUSO. But her father is our father.

NADIA. Now everything is in the past – you do not need to be punished any more.

MAVUSO. My punishment is here.

NADIA. It is more important to live – Do not stay here and punish yourself alone, live with us and you'll find a new life – we will forget what happened – don't betray me!

They start walking. Suddenly MAVUSO *stops, pushes* NADIA *away and says –*

MAVUSO. You must go. Don't come back! Never! Go and don't come back! Sorceress! Witch!! Go!!

20.

NADIA *is in* EZEKIEL*'s arms. She cannot stop crying –*

NADIA. I went to see Mavuso and he rejected me.
Because of the sentence – because you and the judge
decided it was better for him to be facing a prison than
to be in it – he has no future. He is handicapped – He
should have been released – Your idea of justice does
not work. It creates injustice – You thought that prison
will destroy him but now it's you who is destroying
him. You just add suffering to suffering.

EZEKIEL. But he and you are adding suffering to
suffering – You, Nadia, you think only of yourself, and
he, and he has not reached a new understanding – He is
in hell, despair is on his shoulders.

It is harsh – a punishment is always hell – some go
through it and it's gone but nearly nobody does – we
live in a dream – we want to possess one another but
we possess nothing –

Between heaven and hell we are offered purgatory – we
must be purged – The most important is to forgive.
Forgive others and forgive ourselves.

I'm not a moralist – I'm just telling you what I'm going
through in myself, every day.

NADIA. I'll go abroad and I'll study medicine, I will
leave my child in your hands – I cannot take the risk of
polluting her with my guilt. She is innocent. I am not.

21.

MAVUSO *is back, facing the prison.* EZEKIEL *comes to him.*

MAVUSO. Uncle Ezekiel!

EZEKIEL. Nadia has gone abroad. She wants to study medicine. She left the little girl with me. I came here today, but I have to go back quickly, I have to take care of the child.

I saw it all – my brother – his pain when your mother died – and at once, Nadia – replacing her mother in the bed – she was thirteen – he sent you abroad – because he knew that you were in love with her – I knew it too – But you, Mavuso, you were old enough and you said nothing – you prefered your sorrow to forgiveness – you waited for the moment for revenge – but he, your father, he thought that what he was doing was right.

MAVUSO. And you, Uncle, you thought that what he was doing was right? Why didn't you say anything? To go abroad was not my choice – he sent me there because he was jealous – he wanted to get rid of me.

EZEKIEL. It was not to me to judge him. I loved him and you, you will never forget him.

Mavuso it is time now for you to pay.

MAVUSO. What have I been doing here all these years?

EZEKIEL. To pay you have to free yourself. You have learned to survive and you do it very well. But now you must go deeper and deeper in yourself. You must keep

the prison inside you all the time, when you cook,
when you walk, when you drink, when you eat, when
you stay still.

One day you will know that your time here is over,
only you will know, and that day you'll be free to
leave, go back to life and take your place.

EZEKIEL *disappears*.

22.

VISITOR. Few days later, I did what Ezekiel told me – In the desert I saw a big white building – I stopped the car. I followed a path leading to a small hill –

And suddenly I saw him.

He had made a little fire, he was eating, not far off there was a pit, covered by a piece of wood and in front of him the prison.

I approached him, I murmured 'Ezekiel'. As he raised his eyes, the look that came through was shocking in its intensity.

I started to ask him why he was there, and what was the unspeakable crime he had commited, but instead of answering, he invited me to share his meal.

What I saw filled me with nausea – To my shame I said – Thank you, I've already eaten.

His eyes, the look in his eyes, the way he sat facing the prison, will never leave me.

I thought that I was intruding on his silence, so I left.

23.

VISITOR. On my way back I was confronted by a man with an axe. I was afraid. But he looked friendly and said that he worried for the man on the hill. And that it was now ten years that he was here, facing the prison.

I was still a bit afraid of his axe, he smiled –

MAN. Our country is upside down. One day, the director of the prison came to hire me – he asked me if I was able to cut heads with my axe – he had heard that I was a very good tree-cutter. He told me that there were too many prisoners to decapitate and that help was needed. I thought – well why not – cutting trees, cutting heads, I could do it very well and help these people to die.

VISITOR. He said that he helped Mavuso all these years.

Then he went on his knees –

MAN. You have to save him! Go and take him with you.

VISITOR. I replied: I have to go home, I have a plane to catch.

The man was in tears, I felt sorry for him.

24.

NADIA *is with* EZEKIEL. *She is older, dressed like a woman from the city.*

NADIA. I am a doctor now. Uncle, you have been so good to me, you took care of my child all these years. I think that it's time I take her with me. I'm ready.

EZEKIEL. Nadia, your daughter speaks and thinks about Mavuso all the time – his photo never leaves her –

NADIA. I forgot Mavuso, she will forget him too.

25.

MAVUSO *is with the* MAN *of the village.*

MAVUSO. This morning, before the sun rose, a guard came with a prisoner. The guard said: This man has the right to sit beside you.

The prisoner told me – I'm condemned to death – this morning they will cut off my head. Yesterday, they asked me if I had a last wish – I said –Yes, I want to see the sun rise next to the man on the hill.

He sat next to me and we saw the sun rise together.

He had two olives in his hand. He gave me one and ate the other.

I spat out the pip, but the man didn't. I asked him – Why did you swallow the stone? He said – My body will be buried in the earth. So a little olive tree will grow and I will still be alive.

MAN. It's exactly what he told me before I cut off his head this morning.

They are going to destroy the prison. They will start soon. The people from the village are leaving. They have no more work.

What will you do without a prison to look at?

MAVUSO. It will still be there.

26.

Sounds of demolition.

Trucks come and go.

27.

MAVUSO *is studying his father's book. After a long time he closes it.*

MAVUSO. One day I felt that the prison inside me had disappeared. I was ready to leave.

But, before leaving, I wanted to see what I could not see for so many years.

28.

He enters the remains of the prison, and starts to dicover what it had been.

MAVUSO. That must be the courtyard where they could go every day –

There must be the place where they ate.

That must be the chapel.

Here are their cells.

And these ones – the cells of the condemned – where they had to wait for their death –

They are still intact – Here are their graffiti – with their last prayers – their last hopes to see the world change.

Suddenly the MAN *of the village is there.*

What are you doing here?

MAN. I lost my job, no more heads to cut. But you, what are you doing here?

MAVUSO. I am leaving. Do you want to come with me?

MAN. No, this is my home now.

MAVUSO *walks away.*

29.

VISITOR. Few years later, I came back to the foreign country. I wanted to see Ezekiel, there were so many questions I wanted to ask him, but he was not there.

I went back to the desert, I found the path, I found the place.

There was no prison, and there was no prisoner.

The End.

PETER BROOK

Peter Brook is one of the world's best-known theatre directors. Outstanding in a career full of remarkable achievements are his productions of *Titus Andronicus* (1955) with Laurence Olivier, *King Lear* (1962) with Paul Scofield, and *The Marat/Sade* (1964) and *A Midsummer Night's Dream* (1970), both for the Royal Shakespeare Company. Since moving to Paris and establishing the International Centre for Theatre Research in 1970 and the International Centre for Theatre Creation when he opened the Théâtre des Bouffes du Nord in 1974, he has produced a series of events which push at the boundaries of theatre, such as *Conference of the Birds* (1976), *The Iks* (1975), *The Mahabharata* (1985) and *The Tragedy of Carmen* (1981) to name but a few. His films include *Lord of the Flies* (1963), *King Lear* (1970), *The Mahabharata* (1989) *Tell Me Lies* (restored 2013) and *Meetings with Remarkable Men* (restored 2017). His hugely influential books, from *The Empty Space* (1968) to *Tip of the Tongue* (2017), have been published in many languages throughout the world.

MARIE-HÉLÈNE ESTIENNE

Marie-Hélène Estienne joined the Centre International de Créations Théâtrales (C.I.C.T.) in 1977. She was Peter Brook's assistant on *La Tragédie de Carmen*, *Le Mahabharata*, and collaborated to the staging of *The Tempest*, *Impressions de Pelléas*, *Woza Albert!* and *La Tragédie d'Hamlet* (2000). She co-authored *L'homme qui* and *Je suis un phénomène* performed at Théâtre des Bouffes du Nord. She wrote the French adaptation of Can Themba's play *Le Costume*, and *Sizwe Banzi est mort* by Athol Fugard, John Kani and Winston Ntshona. In 2003, she wrote the French and English adaptations of *Le Grand Inquisiteur* (*The Grand Inquisitor*) based on Dostoyevsky's *Brothers Karamazov*. She was the author of *Tierno Bokar* in 2005, and of the English adaptation of *Eleven and Twelve* by Amadou Hampâté Bâ in 2009. With Peter Brook, she co-directed *Fragments*, five short pieces by Beckett, and again with Peter Brook and composer Franck Krawczyk, she freely adapted Mozart and Schikaneder's *Die Zauberflöte* (*The Magic Flute*) into *Une flûte enchantée*. She co-created *The Suit* in 2012 and *The Valley of Astonishment* in 2013, both performed at the Young Vic, London.